Nature All Around
TREES

Written by
PAMELA HICKMAN

Illustrated by
CAROLYN GAVIN

Kids Can Press

For Helen, with love from Nana — P.H.

To the author, Pamela Hickman, for entrusting me to illustrate her wonderful series and to my family, who put up with me during busy design days — C.G.

Acknowledgments

My thanks to Carolyn for her wonderful art. Also, to my editor, Katie Scott, who is a pleasure to work with. — *P.H.*

Big thanks to Katie Scott for finding me and to Karen Powers, the designer, who was full of direction and guidance throughout the project. Both women were full of encouragement and invaluable experience from start to finish. — *C.G.*

Text © 2019 Pamela Hickman
Illustrations © 2019 Carolyn Gavin

Kids Can Press gratefully acknowledges the financial support of the Government of Ontario, through the Ontario Media Development Corporation; the Ontario Arts Council; the Canada Council for the Arts; and the Government of Canada, through the CBF, for our publishing activity.

Published in Canada and the U.S. by Kids Can Press Ltd.
25 Dockside Drive, Toronto, ON M5A 0B5

Kids Can Press is a Corus Entertainment Inc. company

The artwork in this book was rendered in watercolor and gouache.
The text is set in Kepler.

Edited by Katie Scott
Designed by Karen Powers

Printed and bound in Shenzhen, China, in 10/2018 by C & C Offset

CM 19 0 9 8 7 6 5 4 3 2 1

Library and Archives Canada Cataloguing in Publication

Hickman, Pamela, author
    Trees / Pamela Hickman ; illustrated by Carolyn Gavin.

(Nature all around ; 1)
Includes index.
Based on content previously published in The kids Canadian tree book (Toronto: Kids
    Can Press, 1995), and Starting with nature tree book (Toronto: Kids Can Press, 1999).
ISBN 978-1-77138-804-7 (hardcover)

    1. Trees — Canada — Juvenile literature. I. Gavin, Carolyn, illustrator   II. Title.

QK201.H54 2019   j582.160971   C2018-902077-6

Contents

Trees Are All Around

Do you like to climb trees, sit under their shady branches on a hot summer's day, eat apples and peaches, read books or watch birds? If you said yes to any of these, then trees are already an important part of your life.

The United States and Canada are two of the most forested countries in the world. Trees provide food and shelter for wildlife and help to keep the soil, water and air clean. Their wood is used for lumber and paper. No matter where you live, you depend on trees every day. Take a look at the trees throughout these pages and discover how different trees have lots in common.

More than 850 tree species are native to the United States and Canada. Find out how to identify different trees on pages 24–25.

There are two kinds of trees: deciduous and evergreen. Turn the page to find out more!

Trees make their food from sunlight in a process called photosynthesis. See page 9.

Check out the map on pages 20–21 to find out what forest region you live in.

Trees make great homes for a number of animals, such as birds, squirrels and bugs. Take a look at the terrific tree house on pages 22–23.

5

Trees Up Close

Trees are woody plants that grow at least 3 m (10 ft.) tall. Unlike woody shrubs, they have only one stem, or trunk. Trees come in many different shapes and sizes, but they all have some parts in common.

The CROWN is made up of the leaves and branches at the top of the tree.

The TRUNK supports the tree. It carries water and nutrients between the roots and branches.

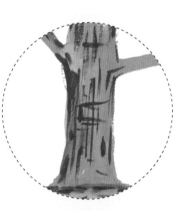

LEAVES make food for the tree from sunlight and clean our air. They shade the ground, cooling the roots below.

BARK protects the trunk and branches from extreme weather, infestation, disease and sometimes even fire.

SEEDS are often found in the tree's fruit or cones. After falling to the ground, a seed can grow into a new tree.

ROOTS suck up water and nutrients from the soil and anchor the tree into the ground.

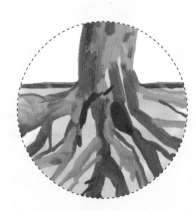

BRANCHES distribute the leaves, exposing them to the most sunlight. They carry water and nutrients to the leaves.

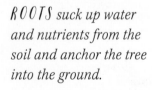

TWO KINDS OF TREES

Have you ever noticed that some trees lose all their leaves in the fall or at the start of the dry season, but other trees stay green all year round? In general, trees that lose their leaves are called deciduous, or broad-leaved. In the spring, they grow new leaves and might have flowers that produce fruit.

Trees that shed only a few leaves at a time are called evergreens. New leaves grow in before all the old ones fall off, so the trees are always green. Most conifers are a type of evergreen that has needles or scales, and cones. Many cones will open so that their ripe seeds can blow away. When it rains, the cones close to keep the seeds dry.

DECIDUOUS

WHITE OAK

EVERGREEN

ENGELMANN SPRUCE

HEMLOCK

DOUGLAS FIR   SCOTCH PINE

STRANGE TREES

Larch trees are two kinds of trees at once. They are coniferous because they have cones instead of flowers. But they are also deciduous since they lose all of their needles in the fall and grow new ones the next spring.

LARCH

🌿 *In the southern United States, some palms and yuccas grow to tree size. But they are more closely related to grasses than to the trees you'll find in this book.*

Looking at Leaves

Leaves come in all different shapes and sizes, and are important clues in identifying trees. Some leaves are whole, or undivided. They are called simple leaves. Compound leaves are divided into small parts called leaflets. Use this page to identify the different trees in your neighborhood by looking at their leaves.

SIMPLE LEAF   COMPOUND LEAF

leaflet

ASH

WHITE BIRCH

AMERICAN SYCAMORE

RED OAK

LINDEN

HICKORY

SUMAC

MESQUITE

SUGAR MAPLE

WEEPING WILLOW

WHY ARE LEAVES GREEN?

A tree's green leaves are filled with a chemical called chlorophyll (CLOR-o-fil). When sunlight hits a leaf, the chlorophyll absorbs the red and blue light, but reflects the green part of the spectrum. You see the reflected light, making the leaf appear green. Chlorophyll plays an important part in making food for the tree in a process called photosynthesis.

🌿 *Turn to page 16 to find out why leaves change color in the fall!*

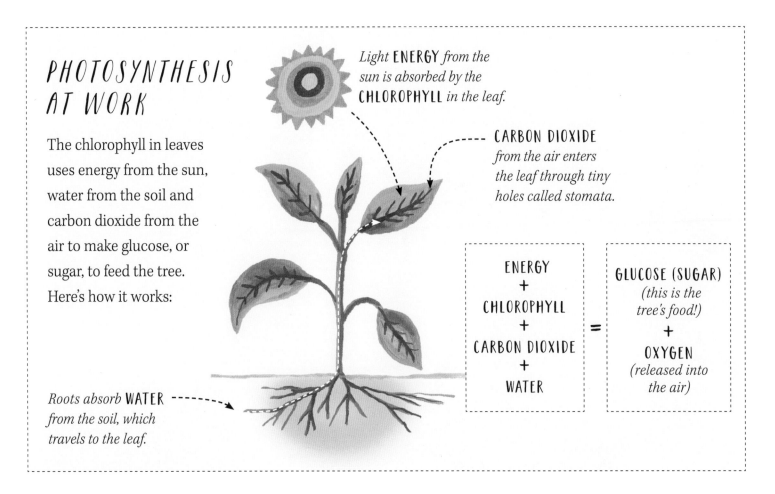

PHOTOSYNTHESIS AT WORK

The chlorophyll in leaves uses energy from the sun, water from the soil and carbon dioxide from the air to make glucose, or sugar, to feed the tree. Here's how it works:

Light ENERGY from the sun is absorbed by the CHLOROPHYLL in the leaf.

CARBON DIOXIDE from the air enters the leaf through tiny holes called stomata.

ENERGY + CHLOROPHYLL + CARBON DIOXIDE + WATER = GLUCOSE (SUGAR) *(this is the tree's food!)* + OXYGEN *(released into the air)*

Roots absorb WATER from the soil, which travels to the leaf.

RESPIRATION

A tree's energy comes from a process called respiration. This involves combining glucose (from photosynthesis) with oxygen and releasing carbon dioxide. This is the opposite of what happens in photosynthesis. Another difference is that trees respire all the time — even in the dark — or they will die, whereas photosynthesis cannot happen in the dark.

FRESH AIR

When leaves take in air during photosynthesis and respiration, they absorb gas pollutants, such as ozone, sulfur dioxide, nitrogen oxide and carbon monoxide. A leaf's surface can also trap tiny pollution particles, removing them from the air. In this way, leaves help to keep our air clean!

A Tree's Life

Most trees start out as seeds. These seeds come from the fruit or cones of "parent" trees. Wind, water and birds or other animals can carry a seed to a new place to grow, where it waits for the right conditions to germinate, or sprout. Watch as this red maple seed turns into a tiny tree in four to six weeks.

🌱 *Find out how mature trees continue to grow on page 14.*

1 *The seed coat, or outer shell, softens. As it absorbs water, the seed cracks open to release the plant inside.*

2 *A tiny root grows down into the soil. It absorbs more water to help the tree grow.*

3 *Two cotyledons, or seed leaves, sprout. They provide the first food for the growing plant.*

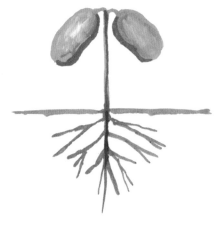

4 *The cotyledons shrink and a pair of new true leaves form at the tip of the shoot.*

5 *The stem continues to grow from the tip, and more pairs of leaves grow out of it. You can start to recognize a small tree.*

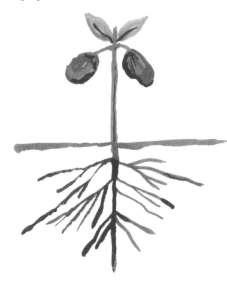
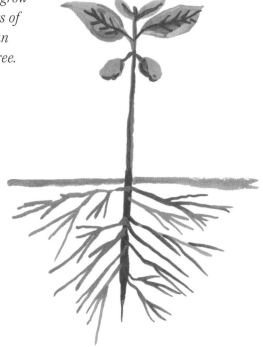

AGING A TREE

You can tell how old a tree was when it was cut down by looking at its stump. Wet the stump to reveal a pattern of light and dark rings. The light rings show the fast spring and early summer growth. The dark rings show the slower growth of late summer and early fall. In most cases, each pair of light and dark rings counts for one year of growth.

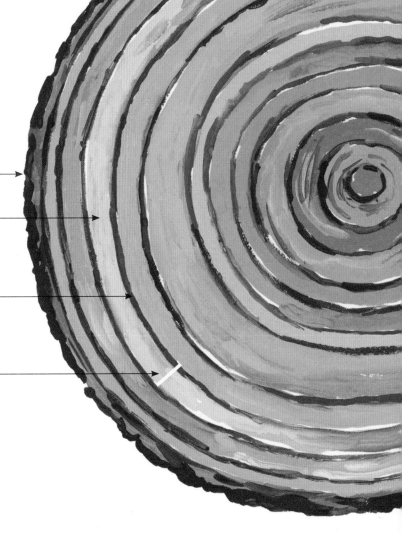

bark

light ring: fast growth in spring and early summer

dark ring: slow growth in late summer and early fall

one year's growth: a pair of light and dark rings

LIFE AFTER DEATH

As strange as it may sound, a dead tree is often very much alive with unseen activity. When a tree dies and falls to the forest floor, it becomes a new habitat for an amazing array of plants, animals and fungi.

Different species live on top of or underneath the log, under the bark or in the wood. Some animals, such as woodpeckers, just visit to feed on the insects living in the log.

Trees in Spring

Although trees have buds all winter long, you sometimes only notice buds once they start to get bigger. When the ground thaws, the tree roots can again suck up lots of water. Water travels up to the buds, causing them to swell and eventually burst open.

Inside a deciduous bud, you might find tiny leaves, flowers or both. When a leaf bud opens, the thicker outer scales usually fall off. The tiny leaves inside unfold, and photosynthesis begins to feed the tree. Instead of flowers, conifer buds open to reveal cones or needles.

MAGNOLIA

POLLINATION

Cones and flowers have to be pollinated to produce seeds. Wind blows a male cone's pollen to a female cone higher up on the tree. The fertilized female cone closes and hardens to protect the seeds that will grow inside. The male cone eventually shrivels and falls off the tree.

Most deciduous trees have flowers that are pollinated by wind or animals, such as birds, insects or bats. Follow the honeybee as it pollinates a pear tree.

1 *A bee visits the pear tree's flower. Tiny grains of pollen from the flower's male part, or stamen, get stuck to the bee's legs and body.*

STAMEN

PISTIL

2 *The bee visits another flower on a different pear tree. Some pollen drops onto the flower's female part, or pistil.*

3 *The pollen grains germinate and release the male reproductive cells. These travel down the pistil to unite with the egg cells inside the flower's ovary. This is called fertilization.*

OVARY

SEEDS

OVARY

4 *Once the flower is fertilized, seeds develop inside the ovary. The rest of the flower falls off the tree.*

5 *The ovary develops into a thick, fleshy covering around the seeds. This is the pear.*

In early spring, most deciduous trees have flowers. Trees such as black cherry plums produce flowers before leaves. So do willows, alders and poplars. This can be an advantage during pollination. Large leaves can crowd flowers, getting in the way of wind or animal pollinators. Some oak and beech trees produce their leaves and flowers at roughly the same time. Others produce their leaves first.

BLACK CHERRY PLUM

Trees in Summer

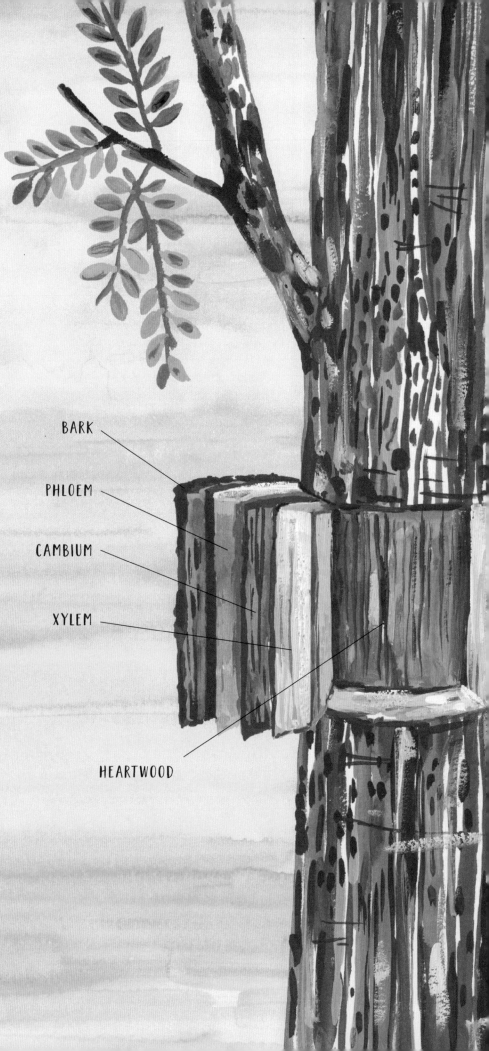

Most of a tree's growth happens during the warm days of summer. Trees grow in two ways: length and width.

A tree grows longer because of special living cells at the tips of the branches and roots. As these special cells divide and lengthen, they push the branches outward and the roots downward.

The trunk and branches grow wider because of a very thin layer of living cells called the cambium. On the outside of the cambium lies the phloem (FLO-em), or inner bark. Food from the leaves is transported to the rest of the tree through tube-like structures in the phloem. As the cambium produces new phloem cells, the old ones get pushed out and crushed, and then die. The dead cells form the tree's bark. On the inside of the cambium lies the xylem (ZIE-lem), or living sapwood. Its tube-like structures carry water and nutrients from the roots up to the leaves. As the cambium produces new xylem cells, the older cells die and turn into heartwood. Most of a tree trunk is made of heartwood.

BARK

PHLOEM

CAMBIUM

XYLEM

HEARTWOOD

14

NUT TREES

During summer, a tree's fruit grows and ripens. A nut is actually a kind of fruit that has a hard shell with a seed inside. True nuts, such as chestnuts, acorns and hazelnuts, have a shell that doesn't open when the nut is ripe. Other things that we call nuts, such as pecans, almonds and walnuts, are actually the large seeds of fruit. They have a softer, fleshy outer layer that usually rots to release the edible seed inside.

ACORN

PECAN

HAZELNUT

WALNUT

ALMOND

CHESTNUT

STRANGE TREES

The largest tree in the world, nicknamed "General Sherman," is a giant sequoia in California's Sequoia National Park. This tree probably started growing about 2000 years ago. Some sequoias live to be 3200 years, so General Sherman is only middle-aged. It is as tall as a 23-story building, and you would have to join hands with 24 of your friends to reach around its trunk!

GIANT
SEQUOIA

Trees in Fall

When the summertime greens of deciduous leaves turn to reds, yellows, oranges and purples, you know that fall has arrived. These colors are actually in the leaves all summer long, but they are hidden by the chlorophyll during photosynthesis. When fall comes, leaves stop making chlorophyll. Soon afterward, the green color disappears and the other colors take over.

Each tree has its own mixture of pigments that gives the leaves their colors. Leaves that have the carotenoid pigments will turn orange or yellow, while ones that have the anthocyanin pigment will turn red or purple. That's why we see so many different colors in the fall.

FALLING LEAVES

When the daylight gets shorter and the cold fall weather sets in, deciduous trees prepare for the coming winter. Just like a hibernating animal, trees rest in the cold months. They also stop growing. Once the ground freezes, the roots can't absorb water from the soil. To survive, the tree must stop water from being lost through the leaves, so a thin layer of cells, like a scab, grows between the tree branch and the leaf. Each leaf is cut off from the tree's supply of water and nutrients, and eventually the leaf falls off the tree.

Unlike deciduous trees, evergreens keep their needles all year round. A thick waxy layer covers the needles and prevents water loss during the colder months. As long as an evergreen has some water and sunlight, it can undergo photosynthesis. But in late fall, when all the water in the ground is frozen, evergreens go dormant until the warmer weather returns.

scab

Bigleaf maples get their name from their enormous leaves. They are the largest leaves of any maple tree species and can grow wider than this page. A bigleaf's bark is special, too. It soaks up water so it is always damp, and this makes it a great place for ferns, mosses and liverworts to grow.

BIGLEAF MAPLE

 A big, old oak tree may drop 700 000 leaves in the fall. In warmer climates, deciduous trees drop their leaves at the beginning of the dry season.

Trees in Winter

In the cold winter months, a deciduous tree's bare branches and grayish-brown or white bark almost make the tree appear dead. If you take a close look at the branches and twigs, though, you will see tiny buds at their tips and along their sides. These buds are like little packages, full of next spring's beautiful leaves and flowers. Buds come in all sorts of shapes, sizes and textures. Many buds are sticky with a waterproof resin that keeps the new leaves inside warm and dry.

This bumpy ring is where the twig started growing last spring. The distance to the end of the twig tells you how much it has grown.

bud

SWEET SAP

In the United States and Canada, sap from sugar maples is used to make delicious maple syrup in late winter and early spring. The sap will flow when daytime temperatures are warmer than 0°C (32°F) but nighttime temperatures are below freezing.

After the sap is extracted from the tree, it must be boiled for several hours. As the water evaporates, the sap becomes darker, thicker and sweeter as it turns into syrup.

COLD REQUIREMENT

Not only can trees survive a cold winter, they actually need the cold before they can grow again in the spring. Each species requires a certain number of cold days during winter. The tree can only start to grow and flower again in spring once it has met its cold requirement. This helps protect the tree from flowering too early in the spring when cold weather could kill the blossoms.

CRACKING TREES

When the winter days feel warmer but the nights are still freezing cold, sometimes cracks appear in trees with thin bark. The bark and inner wood expand a little in the warm sun, especially on the south or west side of the tree. When the sun stops shining, the bark cools quickly and contracts faster than the inner wood. This can cause a crack. The colder the night, the bigger the crack. On really cold nights, you may hear a loud bang when a tree cracks.

Forest Regions

If you were walking through a forest on the west coast of British Columbia, you would see different trees than someone hiking in a forest in Florida. That's because each kind of tree needs its own special combination of soil and climate to grow. Look at the map to find the region where you live.

CANADA

UNITED STATES

ALASKA

HAWAII

HAWAII (UNITED STATES)

Forest Regions	*Main Tree Species*
tropical rain forest	*ʻōhiʻa lehua, koa*
tropical dry forest	*koa, koaiʻa, ʻakoko, ʻōhiʻa lehua, lonomea, māmane, loulu, lama, olopua, wiliwili, ʻiliahi*

Non-Forest Regions	
	scrubland
	mountain bush

Non-Forest Regions

	tundra
	grassland
	desert
	scrubland

CANADA

Forest Regions	Main Tree Species
Acadian	red spruce, balsam fir, yellow birch
boreal	white spruce, black spruce, balsam fir, jack pine, white birch, trembling aspen, tamarack, willow
Carolinian (or deciduous)	beech, maple, black walnut, hickory, oak
coast	western red cedar, western hemlock, Sitka spruce, Douglas fir
Columbia	western red cedar, western hemlock, Douglas fir
Great Lakes–St. Lawrence	red pine, eastern white pine, eastern hemlock, yellow birch, maple, oak
montane	Douglas fir, lodgepole pine, ponderosa pine, trembling aspen
subalpine	Engelmann spruce, subalpine fir, lodgepole pine

UNITED STATES

Forest Regions	Main Tree Species
northern	white pine, jack pine, red pine, eastern hemlock, white spruce, black spruce, balsam fir, yellow birch, sugar maple, trembling aspen, bigtooth aspen, American beech
southeastern	shortleaf pine, longleaf pine, slash pine, loblolly pine, oak, magnolia, tupelo, hickory
central hardwood	black walnut, American sycamore, oak, maple, yellow poplar, ash, sweetgum, hickory, basswood, yellow buckeye
Rocky Mountain	lodgepole pine, ponderosa pine, Douglas fir, Engelmann spruce, trembling aspen, western larch, juniper, western white pine
Pacific coast	Douglas fir, western hemlock, mountain hemlock, cedar, western larch, oak, bigleaf maple, trembling aspen, giant sequoia, redwood, juniper, cypress, sugar pine, ponderosa pine, whitebark pine
subtropical	mangrove, West Indies mahogany, sapodilla

A Terrific Tree House

Trees make terrific homes for many animals, from tiny insects to birds to mammals such as squirrels. A place where an animal lives is called its habitat. All kinds of different animals may share one tree as a habitat, using it for food, shelter and a place to raise their young. Take a look at the animals that call this sugar maple tree home.

HONEYBEE

🍂 *Honeybees feed on flower pollen.*

🍂 *Many bird species, including the white-breasted nuthatch and evening grosbeak, nest in tree holes or build their nests in the branches. They feed on the tree's seeds, sap and buds, or on the insects that also live in the tree.*

EVENING GROSBEAK

PORCUPINE

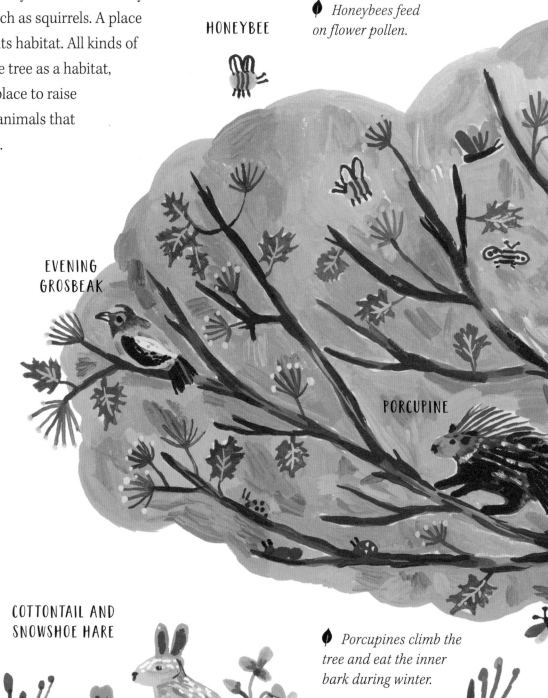

🍂 *Eastern cottontails and snowshoe hares feed on young maple stems and buds, especially in winter when other food is scarce.*

COTTONTAIL AND SNOWSHOE HARE

🍂 *Porcupines climb the tree and eat the inner bark during winter.*

The yellow-bellied sapsucker, a type of woodpecker, drills a distinct pattern of shallow holes in the bark. The holes fill with sap, and the bird laps it up with its brush-like tongue.

Many insects, including ants, wasps and sap beetles, are attracted to the sap wells created by sapsuckers.

WASP

A variety of insects live and feed on sugar maple leaves, including the cecropia moth, gall midges and snout beetles.

CECROPIA MOTH

WHITE-BREASTED NUTHATCH

Red squirrels feed on seeds and buds. They also lick up sap from sapsucker holes.

RED SQUIRREL

YELLOW-BELLIED SAPSUCKER

White-tailed deer and moose eat seedlings, green leaves and woody stems.

WHITE-TAILED DEER

23

Beginner Tree-Watching

Tree-watching is a great year-round hobby no matter where you live. Choose a tree in your neighborhood and watch it throughout the seasons.

Draw pictures or take photos, and make notes of how the tree changes. You can use this checklist and a field guide to trees to help identify your tree.

SILHOUETTES

- What is the general shape of the tree?

columnar   *round*

weeping   *pyramid*

vase

- Is the tree wider at the top or the bottom?
- Is the top pointed or rounded?
- Does it have branches all the way down the trunk?

LEAVES

- Are they broad and flat? Or do they have needles or scales?

broad   *needles*   *scales*

- If broad and flat, what shape are the leaves?

palmate   *lanceolate*   *ovate*   *spatulate*   *cordate*
(palm-shaped) *(spear-shaped)* *(egg-shaped)* *(spoon-shaped)* *(heart-shaped)*

- Are they simple or compound?

simple   *compound*

- If compound, do the leaflets grow opposite or alternate?

opposite   *alternate*

- What color are the leaves in each season?

FLOWERS, CONES AND FRUIT

- Does the tree have cones? What shape and size are they? Where do they grow?

white pine cones

jack pine cones

- Does the tree have flowers? What color, shape and size are they?

cherry blossom

yellow poplar flower

- What color is the ripe fruit? Is it hard like a nut or soft like a cherry?

acorn

gala apple

apricot

- What shape, size and color are the seeds?

BARK

- What color is the bark?
- Is the bark rough or smooth?
- Is it scaly, stringy, flaky, peeling or ridged?

BUDS

- Are the buds pointed or rounded?
- Are they sticky or dry?
- Do the buds smell?
- Do the buds grow opposite or alternate?

BINOCULARS

CAMERA

FIELD GUIDE

NOTEBOOK

PENCIL

25

More Strange Trees

TREES WITH KNEES

SOUTHERN FLORIDA

A mangrove's roots grow underwater, so the tree must send up special "breathing roots" that poke above the mud at low tide. These roots, called knees, take in oxygen and other gases from the air and send them down to the buried roots.

MANGROVE

BEAN TREES

AMERICAN MIDWEST

Beans don't usually grow on trees. But northern catalpa trees produce bean-like seedpods that can be 50 cm (20 in.) long or more. These beans are not for eating, just for growing more catalpa trees.

MANCHINEEL

TOXIC TREES

FLORIDA

All parts of the dangerous manchineel tree contain poisonous chemicals. In the rain, sap from the tree can drip on your skin and cause blistering and other painful sores. The tree's fruit are called "death apples" since they are toxic to anyone who accidentally takes a bite.

CATALPA

CAMOUFLAGE TREES
SOUTHERN ONTARIO AND EASTERN HALF OF THE U.S., SOUTH TO FLORIDA

The American sycamore's bark is not very flexible, so it flakes off in large, irregular sheets as the tree grows. The new bark underneath is a different color, so the trunk looks like a patchwork of greenish-white, brown and gray, similar to a soldier's camouflage uniform.

SYCAMORE

BRISTLECONE PINE

ANTIQUE TREES
UTAH, NEVADA AND EASTERN CALIFORNIA

Unlike most trees, bristlecone pines thrive high up on mountains, where there is dry, shallow soil and cold, strong winds. In fact, they are the world's oldest trees and are known to live over 5000 years. These trees grow very slowly and may be only a few feet tall even after hundreds of years.

LASTING LEAVES
SOUTHERN AND EASTERN CANADA, EASTERN U.S. TO MIDWEST

Even though they are deciduous, oak, beech and hornbeam trees sometimes hang on to their leaves all winter until they are finally blown or broken off in the spring. One idea for why this happens is that the dead leaves protect the buds from hungry animals.

BEECH

Endangered Trees

If an animal is in danger, it can sometimes run away or hide to keep safe. Trees can't protect themselves from attacking insects or disease, logging and construction, or forest fires. Some trees, such as the Florida torreya and the Virginia round-leaf birch, are listed as endangered or threatened, and may die out completely unless something is done to protect them.

Fortunately, some trees are protected in parks and nature reserves. Conservation groups and local governments are also teaching landowners about the need to protect the habitats of these endangered species.

You can help to protect the trees in your neighborhood and across the country by following a few simple steps:

🍃 Never pull off a tree's bark or carve into it. The bark shields the tree from insects, fungi and disease that can hurt or kill the tree. It also protects the cambium, xylem and phloem so the water and nutrients can flow.

🍃 Host a fundraiser for a conservation group that protects trees. Have a tree-themed bake sale or sell tickets for a guided hike led by a naturalist (a nature expert) through a local park or forest.

🍃 Reduce, reuse and recycle products made from trees by

- asking your parents to buy recycled paper

- not using disposable plates and napkins

- choosing products with little or no packaging

- recycling newspapers, writing and computer paper, and cardboard

- writing or printing on both sides of paper

FLORIDA TORREYA

VIRGINIA ROUND-LEAF BIRCH

PLANT A TREE

Planting a tree at home or school is a great activity for Earth Day or Arbor Day. The spring, or end of the dry season, is the best time to plant a tree from seed. Choose a place where the tree will have room to grow and won't be in the way of other activities. Once your tree is planted, water it regularly to make sure it will have a long and happy life!

1 Look on the ground for a sprouted seed from a nearby tree. You can also collect seeds from locally grown fruit or buy them at a garden center.

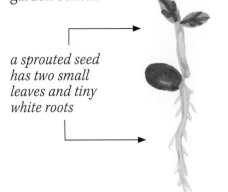

a sprouted seed has two small leaves and tiny white roots

3 Gently place the seed in the hole and cover it with soil. If the seed has already sprouted, be careful not to break off the tiny roots. Keep the green leaves above the soil.

5 If you are planting your seed in a flowerpot on the balcony, put gravel in the bottom of the pot for drainage and then fill the pot with potting soil. Dig a small hole and fill it with water. Plant your seed and cover it with soil. Native trees should be left outside all winter.

2 Dig a hole in the ground, about 15 cm (6 in.) deep. Loosen the soil inside the hole to help the roots spread. Put some compost in the hole and water it.

4 Build a small fence by placing a few sticks, or twigs, in the ground around the hole and winding the rope around the sticks. This will prevent people and animals from stepping on the growing tree.

6 As your tree grows bigger, it may need a tall wooden stake to provide support for its trunk.

Glossary

anthocyanins: the red, purple and blue pigments found in plants

bud: a plant part, often at the tip of a branch, that contains the new year's growth of leaves, flowers or both

cambium: a thin layer of living cells below the outer bark. When these cells divide, they produce new phloem and xylem cells and make the tree thicker.

carotenoids: the yellow and orange pigments found in plants

chlorophyll: the green pigment found in plants

compound leaf: a leaf that is divided into smaller parts called leaflets

cone: the seed-producing part of a coniferous tree

coniferous: a kind of evergreen that produces cones

cotyledon: the first leaf or leaves that come out of a seed when it germinates. They are sometimes called seed leaves.

deciduous: a type of tree that loses its leaves all at once, usually in the fall

dormant: describes a tree that is not growing but is still alive. Trees go dormant in winter when the ground is frozen.

egg cell: the female reproductive cell in a flower or cone. When it unites with the male cell from pollen, it produces a seed.

evergreen: a type of tree that has green leaves all year round

fertilization: the union of a flower's male and female reproductive cells to form a seed

fruit: the hard shell or fleshy part that grows around a developing seed in a flowering plant

glucose: a kind of plant sugar produced during photosynthesis

habitat: the natural home or environment where an animal, plant or other organism lives

heartwood: the non-living woody plant cells in the center of a tree trunk. Heartwood forms the bulk of the trunk.

nut: a fruit with a hard outer shell that doesn't break down to release the seed inside

ovary: the part of the pistil where fertilization takes place. The ovary becomes the tree's fruit.

phloem: the living inner bark that contains the transportation system to take food from the leaves to the rest of the tree. When phloem cells die, they become bark.

photosynthesis: a chemical process in green plants that uses light energy to combine water and carbon dioxide to produce glucose and oxygen

pistil: the female part of a flower made up of the stigma, style and ovary

pollen: a powder-like substance from a flower or male cone that contains a plant's male reproductive cells

pollination: the transfer of pollen from a flower's stamen to another flower's pistil. In coniferous trees, pollen from a male cone lands on a female cone.

respiration: the chemical process that converts glucose and oxygen to carbon dioxide and water to produce energy for the plant. Respiration continues all year round but slows down greatly during winter, when the tree is dormant.

sap: the liquid inside a tree that contains sugars and nutrients dissolved in water

seed: the result of the union of the male and female reproductive cells. Under the right conditions, the cells inside a seed will produce the root and stem of a new plant.

simple leaf: a leaf that is whole and not divided into leaflets

stamen: the male part of a flower made up of the anther and filament

stomata: tiny pores found mainly on the underside of leaves. They open during photosynthesis to let air in and extra water and oxygen out.

xylem: plant tissue that contains tube-like vessels that transport water and nutrients from the roots to the leaves. When xylem tissue dies, it becomes part of the heartwood. Xylem is also known as living sapwood.

Index

A
age of a tree, 11, 15, 27
animals, 4, 5, 10, 11, 13, 22–23

B
bark, 6, 14, 17, 19, 25, 28
    color of, 18, 27
beech trees, 13, 27
birds, 10, 11, 13, 22–23
branches, 6, 14, 18
bristlecone pine trees, 27
buds, 12, 18, 25

C
cambium, 14, 28
catalpa trees, 26
chlorophyll, 9, 16
compound leaves, 8, 24
cones, 6, 7, 10, 12, 13, 25
coniferous trees (conifers), 7, 12. *See also* evergreen trees
conservation, 28

D
death of a tree, 11
deciduous trees, 5, 7, 12, 13, 16, 17, 18

E
endangered trees, 28
evergreen trees, 5, 7, 17. *See also* coniferous trees

F
fall, 11, 16–17
flowers, 7, 12, 13, 25
food
    for trees, 6, 9, 10, 14
    trees as, 4, 19, 22–23
forest regions, 20–21
fruit, 6, 10, 13, 15, 25

G
giant sequoia trees, 15
growth of a tree, 6, 10–11, 14, 17, 19

H
habitats, 4–5, 11, 22–23
heartwood, 14

I
identifying trees, 8, 24–25
insects, 11, 13, 22–23

L
larch trees, 7
leaves, 6, 7, 8–9, 10, 12, 13, 16, 17, 24, 27
life of a tree, 10–11

M
manchineel trees, 26
mangroves, 26
maple syrup, 19
maple trees, 17, 19, 22–23

N
needles, 7, 17, 24
nuts, 15

O
oak trees, 13, 17, 27

P
paper, 4, 28
phloem, 14, 28
photosynthesis, 5, 9, 12, 16, 17
planting a tree, 29
pollen, 13, 22
pollination, 13
pollution, 9

R
respiration, 9
rings (trunk), 11
roots, 6, 10, 12, 14, 17, 26

S
sap, 19, 26
    as food, 22–23
seasons, 11, 12–19
seeds, 6, 7, 10, 13, 15
    as food, 22–23
simple leaves, 8, 24
soil, 4, 6, 9, 17, 20
species of trees, 20–21
spring, 11, 12–13
summer, 11, 14–15
sunlight, 5, 6, 9, 17, 19
sycamore trees, 27

T
tree parts, 6, 14
trunks, 6, 14, 27

W
winter, 18–19, 22

X
xylem, 14, 28